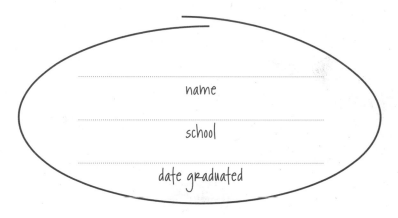

name

school

date graduated

The Next Big Thing

a graduate's journal

CIDER MILL
PRESS

BOOK
PUBLISHERS

Kennebunkport, ME

10-DIGIT ISBN : 1-933662-66-2
13-DIGIT ISBN : 978-1-933662-66-4

This book may be ordered by mail from the publisher. Please include $3.50 for postage and handling.
Please support your local bookseller first!

Books published by Cider Mill Press Book Publishers are available at special discounts for bulk purchases in the United States by corporations, institutions, and other organizations. For more information, please contact the publisher.

Cider Mill Press Book Publishers
"Where good books are ready for press"
12 Port Farm Road
Kennebunkport, Maine 04046

Visit us on the web!
www.cidermillpress.com

Text and design by Debbie Berne,
Herter Studio LLC, San Francisco

Printed in Thailand by Imago

1 2 3 4 5 6 7 8 9 0

Today is a day to remember.

Maybe you've just taken your final, final exam; or had your first summer swim; or started your first full-time job. Maybe you've moved permanently out of your parent's house, or temporarily back in. Maybe you've broken up with your longtime sweetheart or had the worst interview of your life. Maybe you've simply spent the day looking at magazines and walking around the block and wishing you could see into the future. Whatever happened: remember this day.

And tomorrow too.

Because sometime in that hard-to-envision future, you'll want to remember how it felt to be where you are *right now*. Celebrating your graduation, basking in your accomplishments, and squinting into the future with anticipation and probably a little fear.

And that's what this journal is for—to record, reminisce, remember when, think ahead, dream a little, chart a course. It's the place for you to mark this moment of transition while everything is still so alive in your mind. It's the place to acknowledge what's really going on beyond the toasts and congratulations. And it's the place to close your eyes and try to picture yourself six months from now, next year this time, in five years, in twenty-five. Who is that fifty-year-old you and what are you up to? While, of course, there's no possible way of knowing all that will happen to, around, and within you as you move out into the world, there's a lot to be said for pausing a moment to really consider what you care about, what you're interested in, and the future you'd most like to live. It may not get you there, but at least you can begin by pointing in the right direction.

So think big, but keep it in perspective. It may feel like the choices you are making right now will start you down a path from which there's no turning back. And you're right, of course. And yet you'll find that there are many, many, many forks in the long road of an adult life. There are so many more choices to be made. So take a first step. Even a second. But don't worry it unduly. Anytime you want to make a sudden swerve to the left, you can.

So say good-bye to high school, or college, or tech school, or grad school, or med school, or beauty school, or wherever you've been racking up all that good, useful knowledge. It's all out there waiting for you. Say hello to the *next* big thing.

WHAT'S NEXT

SOURCES of INSPIRATION

But wait! What *is* your next big thing? If you're not sure, or you're intimidated by the many choices before you, go back to basics and start with things that really move you. Music, movies, books, politics, religion, art, the environment, technology, your friends, your friends's friends, something you read in the newspaper or see on TV—any of these sources of inspiration can be a great guide and motivator. Instead of worrying about what you *should* do, fantasize a little about what you'd most *like* to do next, and use the following pages to consider some of your options. But first things first: Make a list of the things that really inspire you.

WHERE to go

In some cultures, taking a year to see the world is a rite of passage for many young people. Nothing beats travel to expand your knowledge, your palette, and your empathy for your fellow men and women. Whether you have the yen (and the resources) to visit your state's parks, the great cities of the world, or the remotest mountain village, traveling off your own beaten path can be as meaningful and eye opening as your favorite class or your first job. Take a moment to wonder where you might go.

Istanbul

Alaska

Rome

Cairo

Montana

Moscow

Bangkok

New York City

London

Kyoto

Big Sur

New Orleans

Tel Aviv

Cape Town

Marrakesh

Goa

Tijuana

Costa Rica

Marfa

Amsterdam

Sofia

Athens

Papua New Guinea

Shanghai

Cuba

Cannes

Maine

Ghana

Rio de Janeiro

Nova Scotia

your own backyard

where else?

WAYS to CONTRIBUTE

Build houses with Habitat for Humanity or build schools in Nepal.
Volunteer your business acumen to a local nonprofit or your Saturday
morning to clean up a local park. Donate ten percent of your earnings to
your favorite charity or your old prom dress to the Glass Slipper Project.
Spend an afternoon a week playing basketball with teens or talking with
senior citizens. Run in the Race for the Cure or march on Washington
for a cause you believe in. Considering your skills, time, and inclinations,
ponder what ways you might give back, give to, or give away.

WHAT to BE

Even if you haven't known what you've always wanted to be since grade school, you've probably begun thinking about it now. Approach this process as an adventure, rather than a chore, and don't be afraid to dabble. Let what you've written about in the previous pages help guide you toward a meaningful and exciting next step. And remember: One-third of your life is spent sleeping; one-third spent eating lunch, going to the dentist, and watching TV; when you decide what to do with that final precious third, be sure it makes you happy.

CHART your COURSE

this summer

....

....

....

....

....

....

....

....

....

....

....

....

....

....

....

....

....

....

this year

in five years

{ Commencement speech 1987 · Tufts University }

Whatever you want to do, do it now. For life is time, and time is all there is.

GLORIA STEINEM

Don't be afraid to take a
big step if one is indicated;
you can't cross a chasm in
two small jumps.
DAVID LLOYD GEORGE

You cannot help but learn
more as you take the world
into your hands. Take it up
reverently, for it is an old
piece of clay, with millions
of thumbprints on it.

JOHN UPDIKE

Remember yourself, from the days when you were younger and rougher and wilder, more scrawl than straight line.

ANNA QUINDLEN

Don't live down to
expectations. Go out
there and do something
remarkable.
WENDY WASSERSTEIN

Do not seek to follow in
the footsteps of the wise.
Seek what they sought.
MATSUO BASHO

{ Commencement speech 1997 · Wellesley College }

Every life speaks to the power of what can be done.

OPRAH WINFREY

The important thing is not
to stop questioning.
ALBERT EINSTEIN

Throw your dreams
into space like a kite,
and you do not know what
it will bring back, a new
life, a new friend, a new
love, a new country.
ANAIS NIN

{ Commencement speech 2004 · William and Mary }

Love what you do.
Get good at it.

JON STEWART

Do not follow where the
path may lead.
Go, instead, where
there is no path
and leave a trail.
RALPH WALDO EMMERSON

May you live
every day of your life.
JONATHAN SWIFT

My hope is that
you will not be content
just to be successful
in the way that our society
measures success;
that you will not obey
the rules, when the rules
are unjust; that you will
act out the courage
that I know is in you.

HOWARD ZINN

Success isn't a
result of spontaneous
combustion. You must
set yourself on fire.
ARNOLD H. GLASOW

Live as if your were to die
tomorrow. Learn as if you
were to live forever.
MAHATMA GANDHI

{ Commencement speech 2005 · University of Maine }

Acknowledge your good fortune by sharing it.

STEPHEN KING

> To accomplish great
> things, we must not only
> act, but also dream; not
> only plan, but also believe.
> ANATOLE FRANCE

We must be willing to
let go of the life we have
planned, so as to have the
life that is waiting for us.
E.M. FORSTER

One of the greatest feelings in life is the conviction that you have lived the life you wanted to live—with the rough and smooth, the good and the bad—but yours, shaped by your own choices, and not someone else's.

MICHAEL IGNATIEFF

Some men see things
as they are and ask why.
Others dream things
that never were and
ask why not.
GEORGE BERNARD SHAW

We cannot live only for
ourselves. A thousand
fibers connect us with
our fellow men.
HERMAN MELVILLE

{ Commencement speech 2001 · Mt. Holyoke College }

Believe that the sort of life you wish to live is, at this very moment, just waiting for you to summon it up.

SUZAN-LORI PARKS

Education is the most powerful weapon which you can use to change the world.
NELSON MANDELA

The true meaning of
life is to plant trees,
under whose shade you do
not expect to sit.
NELSON HENDERSON

I hope
you will find
some way
to break the rules
and make
a little trouble
out there.

NORA EPHRON

Growth itself contains
the germ of happiness.
PEARL S. BUCK

PEOPLE I NEVER
WANT TO FORGET

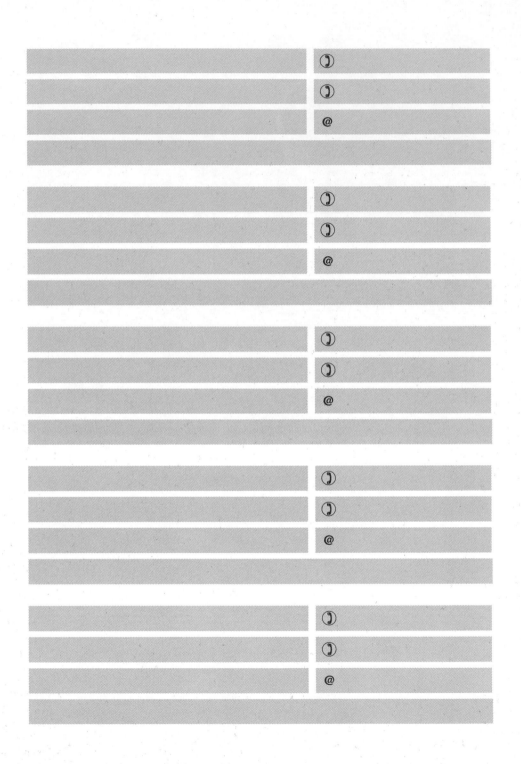

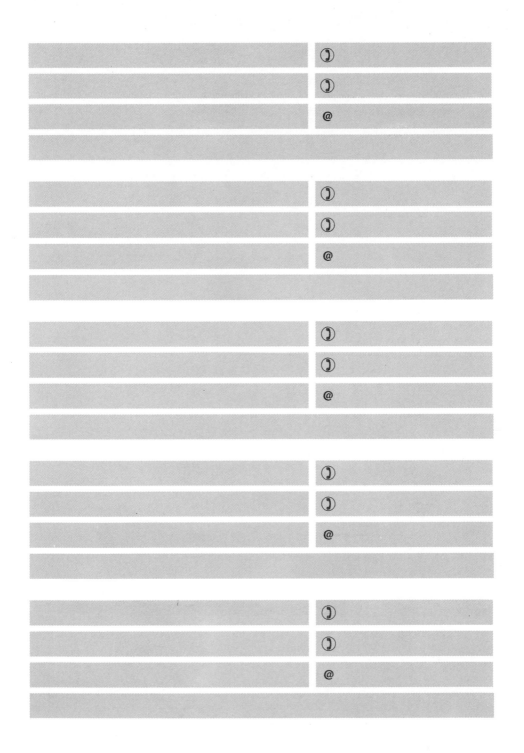

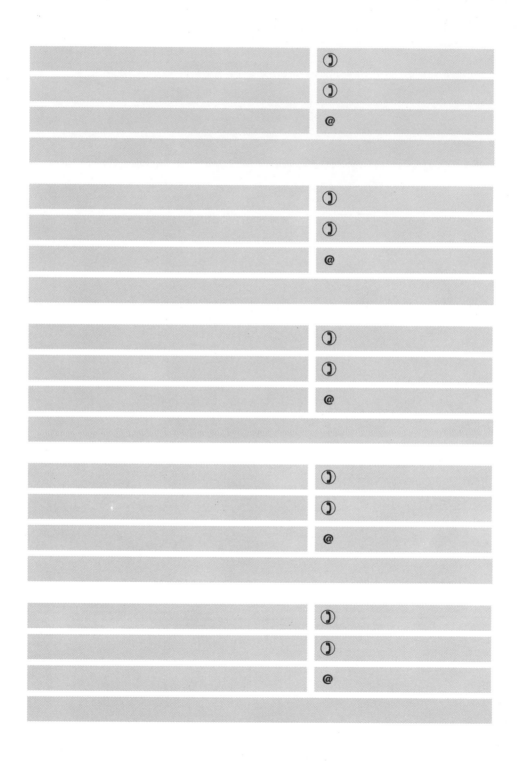

MORE INSPIRATION

As you move out into the world, you will undoubtedly find inspiration in your own individual history. Everything you've done and been up until now has not only prepared you for the future, but will be coming along for the ride. Use the following pages to paste, tape, staple, and paper-clip ephemera that you want to remember, keep, and refer to for inspiration: photos, tickets, notes, artwork, and anything else you treasure.